AINSLEY,

AS YOU GROW EYER OLDER and WISER, MAY YOU
ALSO HAVE OPPORTUNITY TO LEARN ABOUT SUCH
"WONDERS of THE WORLD" AS WELL AS TO VISIT
SOME of THEM.

MERRY CHRISTMAS 2017

Goma and TBD

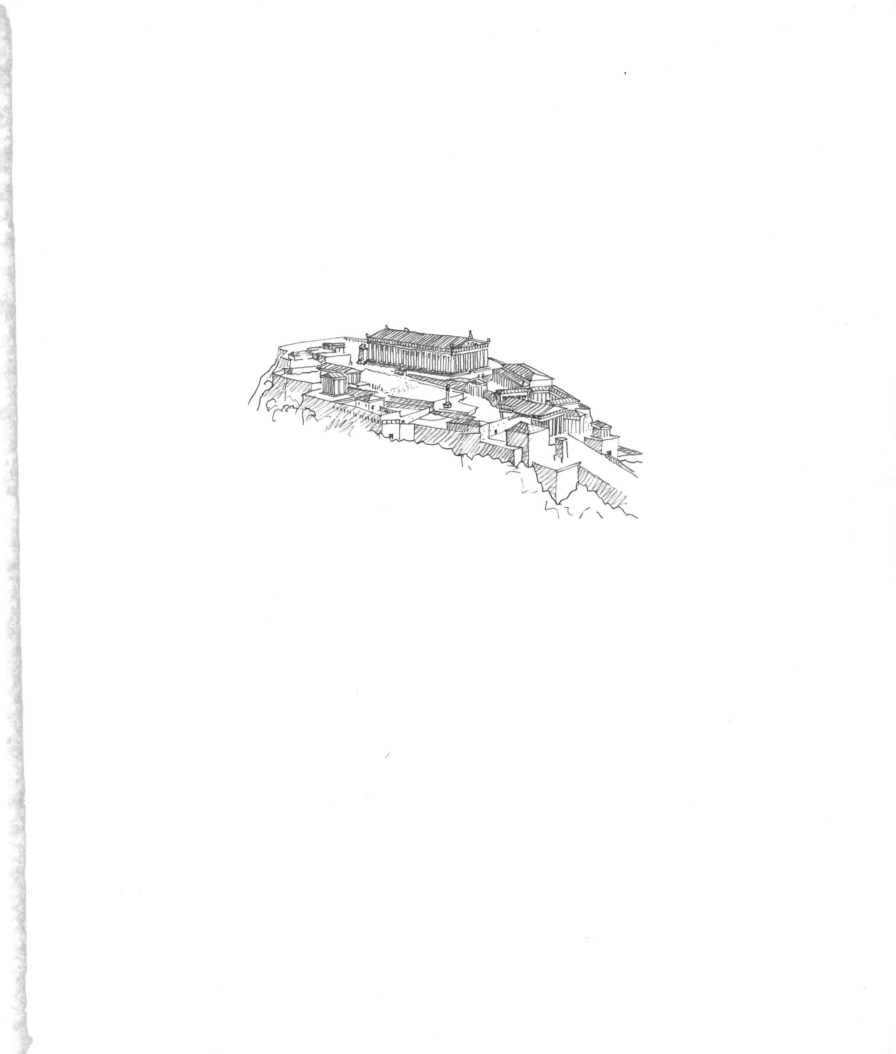

13 Buildings
Children Should Know

Annette Roeder

PRESTEL

Munich · London · New York

Contents

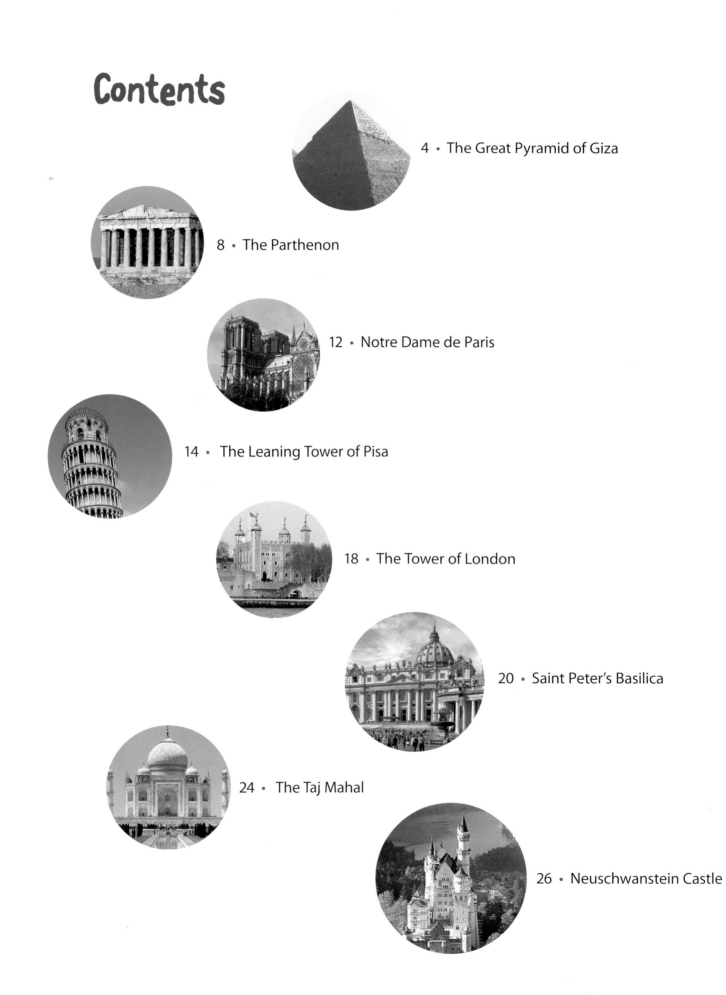

Wasps build their homes out of paper; birds make complicated nests; and moles dig systems of burrows that have lots of rooms. And what about humans? We, too, are born with a need to build things, as you can see if you watch children playing in a sandpit! Unlike most animals, however, humans have come up with a variety of architectural styles over time. Luckily, a lot of great buildings, some of them very old, have been preserved. 13 very special ones are presented and explained to you in this book. It wasn't easy to choose just 13—there are of course many, many more!

✸ The wheel is invented

Baked and glazed tiles first made
in Mesopotamia ✸

| 4000 BCE | 3900 BCE | 3800 BCE | 3700 BCE | 3600 BCE | 3500 BCE | 3400 BCE | 3300 BCE | 3200 BCE | 3100 BCE | 3000 BCE | 2900 BCE |

The Pyramids

were already being
studied a long time ago:
even Napoleon sent
a team of scientists to
Egypt.

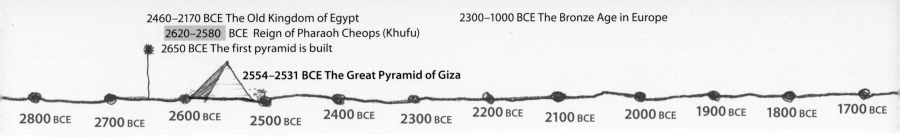

2460–2170 BCE The Old Kingdom of Egypt
2620–2580 BCE Reign of Pharaoh Cheops (Khufu)
2650 BCE The first pyramid is built
2554–2531 BCE The Great Pyramid of Giza
2300–1000 BCE The Bronze Age in Europe

2800 BCE 2700 BCE 2600 BCE 2500 BCE 2400 BCE 2300 BCE 2200 BCE 2100 BCE 2000 BCE 1900 BCE 1800 BCE 1700 BCE

The Great Pyramid of Giza

The only one of the Seven Wonders of the Ancient World to have survived to this day; it is the biggest single building ever to have been constructed—and it was the highest in the world for the longest time. The Great Pyramid of Giza has broken lots of records!

To this very day, we don't quite know how the Egyptians managed to construct this enormous, perfect geometric miracle in stone over 4,000 years ago. You can still visit it on the outskirts of Cairo, the Egyptian capital. What were the pyramids built for? How did the architects and laborers manage to pile the incredibly heavy stones on top of each other without the help of modern machines or electric power? No wonder that some people's imaginations run wild when it comes to this wonder of the ancient world: some talk about a huge observatory, of places of worship and of aliens who could move objects using nothing but the strength of their willpower.

Started: c. 2554 BCE
Location: Giza, near Cairo, Egypt
Commissioned by: Pharaoh Khufu
Height: 146.6 m (481 feet); today, it is only 138.7 m/455 feet high because the tip is missing
Length of each side: 230.3 m (755 feet)
Material: Limestone
Special features: Together with its two sister pyramids, this is the only one of the Seven Wonders of the Ancient World left today

1 Great Pyramid of Giza
2 Entrance
3 Boat pits
4 Temple
5 Covered walkway
6 Queens' pyramids
7 Surrounding wall

The Great Pyramid of Giza

was the main structure on a big burial site that had walls, temples and smaller pyramids for the queens. The Ancient Egyptians even dug pits for the big boats that would carry the dead pharaoh's soul into the afterlife.

5

The archeologists* were right after all. They always thought that the Great Pyramid of Giza was built as a monumental tomb for the pharaoh Khufu, who was called Cheops in Greek. A stone coffin, known as a sarcophagus, was eventually found in the inner chamber. And there can be little doubt that the pyramid was built using the muscle-power of thousands and thousands of laborers and oxen.

Cross-section*

Here, you can see what sorts of rooms or chambers there are inside the Great Pyramid. They are very small even though the structure is so huge!

1   Original entrance

2   Entrance used today

3   Stones blocking the passage

4   Subterranean chamber

5   Queen's chamber

6   Grand gallery

7   King's chamber

8   Weight-relieving chambers

9   Shafts

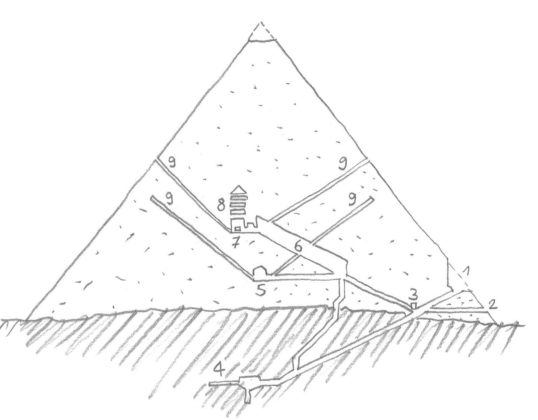

A Big Building for a Small Mummy

For the Ancient Egyptians, life was the journey you had to take to reach your goal: the afterlife. The long path from the valley temple to the pyramid temple and the buried boats are symbols for this journey.

The body of the dead pharaoh was mummified using complicated methods. Specialists dried the body out, removed the inner organs and the brain, and then wrapped the body in a sort of fabric bandage. This way, the dead body would remain

intact in the sarcophagus for eternity. Tests have shown that the pyramids' geometric shape helps speed up mummification.

The mummy of the pharaoh Khufu has disappeared and nothing but this small statue shows us what he looked like when he was alive.

An Army of Laborers or Aliens?

Most experts on pyramids think that approximately 20,000 laborers took 20 years to pull the heavy stones into place using sleds on flat ramps*. On average, these granite slabs weigh 2.5 tonnes, while some of the stone ceiling beams are estimated to weigh 80 tonnes! As a comparison: a family car weighs about 1.5 tonnes.

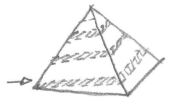

It is possible that ramps wound their way up inside the pyramid, a bit like a snail's shell. This would have protected the workers from the sun's glaring heat.

According to another theory, there was a long, straight ramp leading up the pyramid. The stones of which it was built could then have been incorporated into the pyramid itself, which would explain why there aren't any left for us to see today.

And then there are others who think that the pyramid must have been build by aliens from outer space.

What do you think?

Over the centuries, tomb robbers have stolen everything and anything that could be carried away, including the polished white limestone which formed a casing around the pyramid. They used this stone to build their own houses. That is why the Great Pyramid of Giza now has a stepped outer surface.

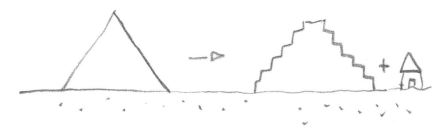

Quiz
A pyramid is a geometric form that has a rectangular base and four identical triangular sides. Where—apart from your math book—can you find other pyramids?
(Answer on p. 46)

Tip
If you log onto www.pbs.org/wgbh/nova/pyramid/explore/khufutomb-kinglo.html, you can go on a virtual exploration of the Great Pyramid of Giza.

2300 BCE–1000 BCE
Bronze Age in Europe

1000 BCE–500 CE Antiquity*

500–432 Phidias
490–429 Pericles

120 BCE
The Romans
first use
cement for
building

970 BCE First evidence of a
pulley system being used

447–432 BCE Parthenon

| 1200 BCE | 1100 BCE | 1000 BCE | 900 BCE | 800 BCE | 700 BCE | 600 BCE | 500 BCE | 400 BCE | 300 BCE | 200 BCE | 100 BCE |

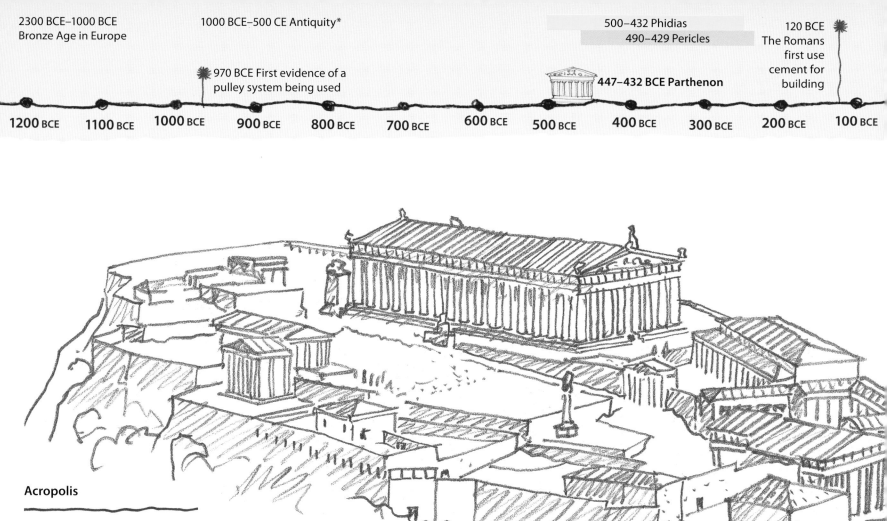

Acropolis

The Acropolis looked
something like this. From
the monumental gate-
way, the propylaea, you
can see the whole of the
Parthenon temple.

The Parthenon temple

And this is what the
Parthenon temple looks
like today. The ruins give
an idea of its former glory.

8

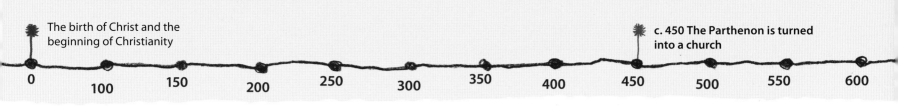

The Parthenon

A colorful temple: the Parthenon is the most famous temple of Greek Antiquity

The buildings on the Acropolis, the "Sacred Rock" of Athens, had been destroyed by the Persians during the Persian Wars. And so the city's governor* Pericles commissioned the famous sculptor Phidias and two architects to redesign the complex. At its center was the biggest and most beautiful of Greek temples: the Parthenon, which is roughly the same size as a soccer pitch.

Although all temples of this period are quite similar, architects constantly tried to improve the rigidly de-fined design of the building to achieve a perfect harmony. To this end, they used cleverly-devised proportions* and little tricks that are not immediately apparent. The corner pillars, for example, are slightly thicker than the rest, because they are better-illuminated than the others, which makes them look thinner. Thanks to this trick, all of the pillars look exactly the same.

There was a 12-meter (39-foot) statue of the goddess Athena in the inner chamber of the Parthenon, in the so-called "cella", that disappeared however shortly after completion.

Started:
447–432 BCE
Location:
Athens, Greece
Architects:
Iktinos and Kallikrates, under the supervision of the sculptor Phidias
Size:
30.8 m x 69.5 m (101 x 228 feet)
Height of outside pillars:
10.43 m (34.2 feet)
Material:
Marble
Style:
Greek Antiquity*
Special features:
Made entirely of marble, including the roof tiles

Sculptures from the Parthenon frieze

The Parthenon was decorated on the inside and the outside with wonderful sculptural reliefs. Only a fraction of these have sruvived to this day and are now scattered in various museums.

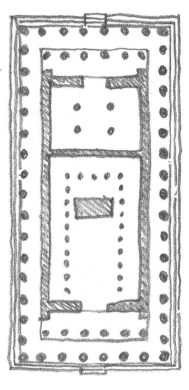

Ground plan*

There were lots of pillars around the "cella", the inner chamber in which the goddess's statue once stood.

The goddess Athena

It has only recently been discovered that Greek temples and statues were painted in bright colors. Tiny fragments of color have shown up under ultraviolet light. The figures' clothes and shields were decorated with colorful patterns, and pictures of animals or battle scenes.

What colors would you paint this statue of Athena?

Three Types of Columns

Classical Antiquity can be divided into three main "orders": Doric, Ionic and Corinthian. The difference becomes clear when you look at the columns.

Doric

Ionic

Corinthian

Doric columns are the only ones that don't have a base. The top end, called the capital, is very plain.

The capital of an ionic column is in the shape of two thick scrolls.

Corinthian columns, on the other hand, are decorated with leaves.

You can impress people if you can remember this!

Quiz
Is the Parthenon a Doric, Ionic or Corinthian temple? (Answer on p. 46)

Tip
You don't even need to go to Greece to see these sorts of columns. A lot of buildings in European cities were built in the neoclassical* style. Munich's Königsplatz square, for example, was inspired by Greek architecture. Is there a building in your city that was built according to a Classical model?

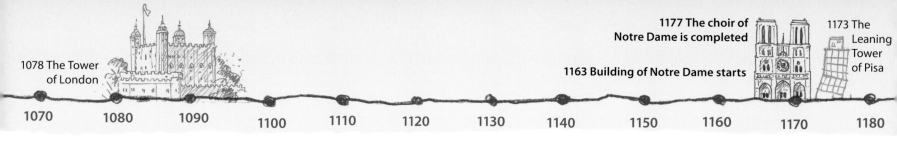
Notre Dame de Paris

Notre Dame in Paris was the model for many famous Gothic cathedrals.

Started:
1163
Location:
Paris, France
Architects:
Jean de Celles and
Pierre de Montreuil
Length:
130 meters (426 feet)
Width:
48 meters (157 feet)
Interior height:
up to 35 meters
(105 feet)
Height of towers:
69 meters (226 feet)
Style: Gothic*
Special features:
Regarded as the model
of all Gothic cathedrals*

Bishop Sully of Paris wanted to build a cathedral in the very latest fashion, so he simply had the previous church demolished—even though it had only just been renovated. He wanted an ultra-modern Gothic church. When the foundation stone of Notre Dame was laid, it became the model for countless other cathedrals.

Notre Dame was the setting for many famous events. Joan of Arc was condemned to death here; Mary Queen of Scots was married in the cathedral; and Napoleon's coronation also took place in Notre Dame.

During the French Revolution the heads of the 28 statues of kings on the main West Front were knocked off, because the rioting mob was angry at all aristocrats. After that, the church was used as a wine store. And if Victor Hugo had not written the famous story of Quasimodo, the Hunchback of Notre Dame, this wonderful building might have fallen into rack and ruin.

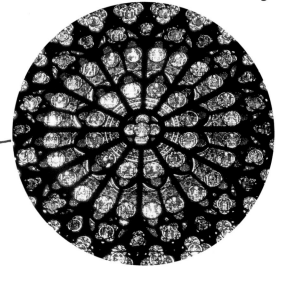

The beautiful stained-glass window

with a diameter of
12 meters (39 feet) is one of
the largest in Europe. A
window like this is called a
"rose window" because it
looks like a flower.

Flying buttresses

are a typical feature of
Gothic buildings. They
help to take the heavy
weight of the roof
off the walls, making
it possible to put in
large windows.

12

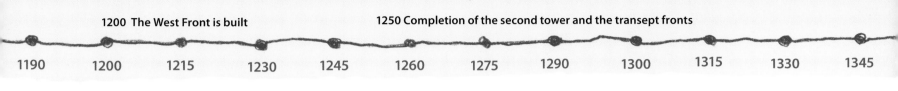

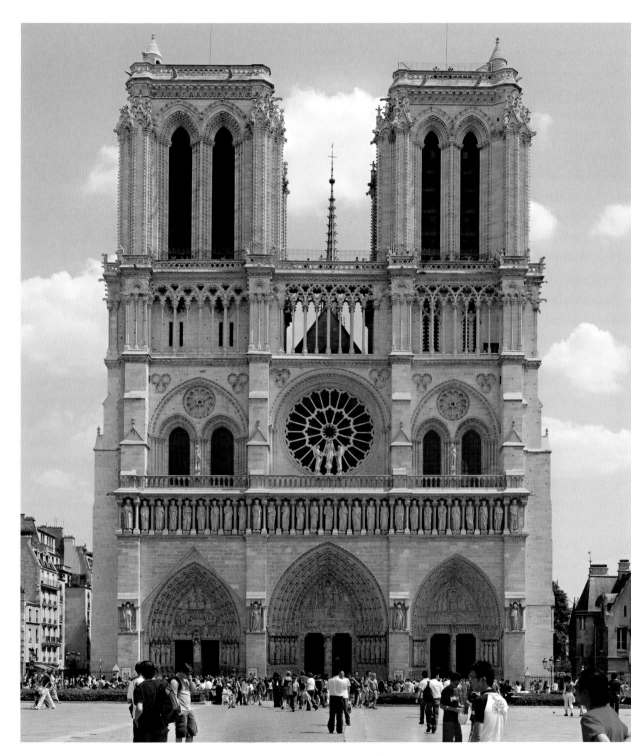

The great West Front

was built slightly asymmetrically* on purpose, so that it did not look too boring. What differences can you spot?

Ground plan

There is usually a special word used to describe most church designs. Notre Dame is a five-naved basilica*.

These funny creatures are called gargoyles. They keep the rainwater away from the church wall. What sort of face would you give your gargoyle?

13

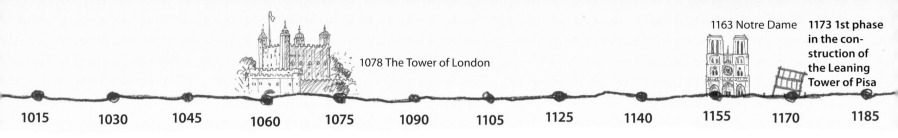

Pisa's bell tower (called a campanile in Italian)

The people of Pisa wanted a really special tower: higher than all the other towers in Italy, and round, too! But what has made it the most famous tower in the world?

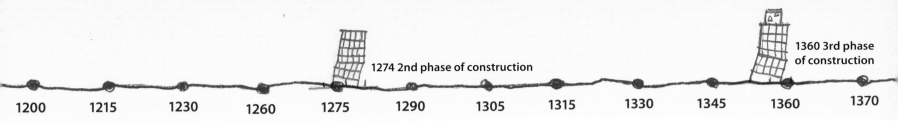
The Leaning Tower of Pisa

The bell tower has stood on Pisa's Cathedral Square for more than 800 years. That is not even a particularly long time: some buildings are much older. And yet every additional year is a little miracle when it comes to this bell tower because it has continued to defy gravity!

Started:
  August 9, 1173
Location:
  Pisa, Italy
1st architect:
  Bonanno Pisano
  1173–84,
  Floors 1–3
2nd architect:
  Giovanni di Simone
  1274–84,
  Floors 4–7
3rd architect:
  Tommaso Pisano
  1360, belfry
Height:
  54 m (177 feet)
Style:
  Romanesque*
Special features:
  The tower leans at an
  angle of 4.43°

When the people of Pisa laid the foundation stone of their campanile, they actually wanted to build the tallest bell tower in Italy that would be a visible sign of their wealth and success. And if there were trouble with the neighbors, the well-off at least could take refuge there. It was to be 100 meters (328 feet) high. When they were building the third level, the laborers had to take to their heels very quickly: the ground gave way on one side and their great tower seemed about to fall over!

If you want to build high in the sky, you must first make sure that you have a solid foundation* that will bear the entire building's weight—but the architect in Pisa hadn't thought of that. And so the thin bottom plate and the first three floors sank about 4 meters (13 feet) into the ground.

The local people were so shocked that they took a 100-year break from building. Then they built the next four floors. The new architect—not the one who had started work on the tower, of course—attempted to balance out the tilt, but that didn't really work, and the tower leaned further and further to one side.

Site plan

The tower ① stands at a small distance from the cathedral ②. You can also see the baptistry ③ on this site plan.

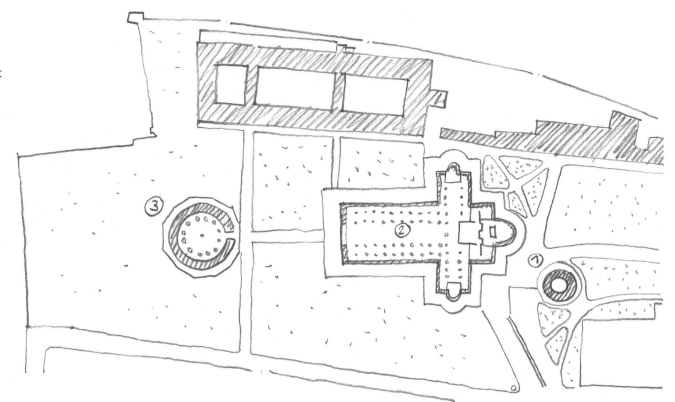

① CAMPANILE

As the tower had still not toppled over a hundred years after that, its third and final architect constructed a belfry on top of it, like a little crown. On one side, two steps lead up to it. On the other, you have to climb four steps. If only they had used a plumb line*!

They have tried again and again to straighten it out, but nobody has quite managed. And that is why the Leaning Tower is as crooked as a banana, as well as leaning to one side!

30 columns

surround every floor. Can you work out how many columns there are altogether?

How would you have designed the belfry that houses the seven bells? Draw your own top floor on top of the tower!

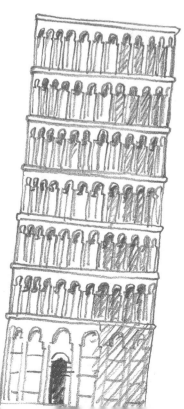

16

Teetering on Tiptoe

The tower really did need a bit of help: leaning further and further to one side over the centuries, the tower had to be closed to visitors in 1990. The risk that it could topple over and bury people underneath it was just too great!

Have you ever tried to move a tower made of building blocks into another position without it collapsing? What would you do? First, 18 steel rings were placed around the tower. One side of the foundation was weighed down with 800 tons of lead weights. That brought the leaning tower 2.5 cm closer to being straight, but looked very ugly.

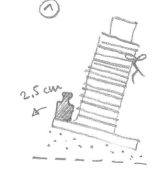

A ring of concrete was then to be poured around the foundation and anchored to the ground. Before doing this, they had to stop the groundwater rising—and it was decided to freeze it. But do you know what happens when water turns to ice? It expands! The tower began to wobble and it looked as though its end might have been near!

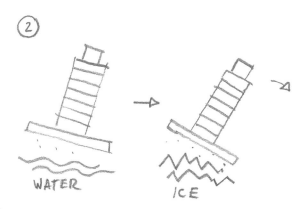

Sometimes, the simplest solution is the best: finally, 50 m³ (1766 ft³) of soil and mud were dug out, very carefully, from underneath the bottom plate on one side. It was almost a miracle: the Leaning Tower of Pisa came 44 cm (17 inches) closer to being straight!

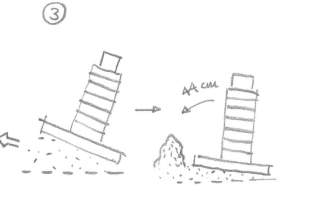

Quiz
How high is the Leaning Tower of Pisa today?
(Answer on page 46)

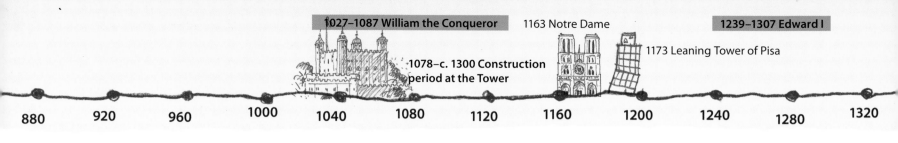

The Tower of London

Started:
1078 (The White Tower completed)
Construction period:
Over 300 years
Location:
London, England
Commissioned by:
William the Conqueror
Height:
White Tower: approx. 30 meters (98 feet)
Total area:
approx. 18 acres
Style: Norman
Material: Stone
Special feature:
6 ravens as permanent residents

With its countless tales both true and made up, the Tower of London is a perfect fairy-tale royal castle.

When William the Conqueror had the first stone building constructed in the 11th century to replace a wooden fort on the site, life for the people of London was still far from easy. This first building, the White Tower, still forms the heart of the complex, although a number of other buildings were added over the centuries.

In the olden days, the Tower was a royal palace; today it houses a display of historic weapons and armory, as well as England's most precious treasure: the Crown Jewels.

The Tower was also a prison, and being "sent to the Tower" often meant death. The first prisoner, however, managed to escape over the wall using a rope which had been hidden in a wine barrel, while his drunken guards were fast asleep and snoring loudly. Other prisoners were not so lucky and many were executed in the Tower. Today people can visit the castle and discover its fascinating history.

Ravens

There have been at least six ravens in the Tower for centuries. They are well looked after and all have names. As legend has it, as long as there are ravens in the Tower, the United Kingdom will not fall!

Tip

If you apply 6–8 weeks in advance, you can be present at the Ceremony of the Keys which takes place every evening at seven minutes to ten. The tradition is over 700 years old and is thought to be the oldest ceremony in England. On the website http://www.hrp.org.uk/TowerOfLondon/WhatsOn/ceremonyofthekeys.aspx you can apply for a pass, which is issued free of charge.

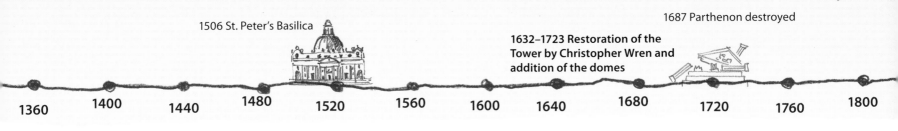

The Tower from the Thames

The light-colored stone, brought across from Normandy in France to build the White Tower, gave the main building in the complex its name.

St. John's Chapel

built in 1080, St. John's Chapel is the oldest surviving Norman chapel.

1 White Tower

2 Waterloo Barracks

3 Scaffold site

4 Chapel

5 Traitors' Gate

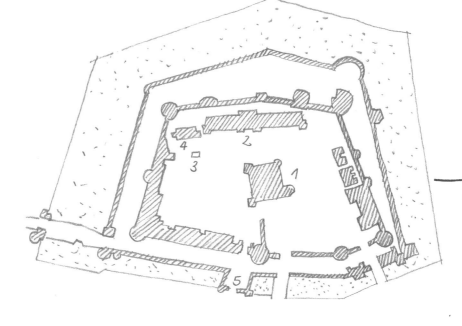

Ground plan

Two circular walls and a moat protect the precious Crown Jewels, which can be viewed on the ground floor of the Waterloo Barracks.

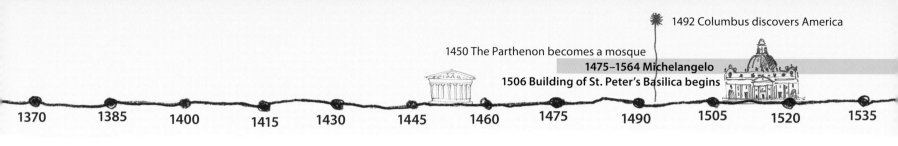

1450 The Parthenon becomes a mosque

1492 Columbus discovers America

1475–1564 Michelangelo

1506 Building of St. Peter's Basilica begins

1370   1385   1400   1415   1430   1445   1460   1475   1490   1505   1520   1535

St. Peter's Basilica

Seen from the outside, it is difficult to see just how enormous St. Peter's Basilica really is. Above the front entrance is the small balcony from which the Pope gives his blessing.

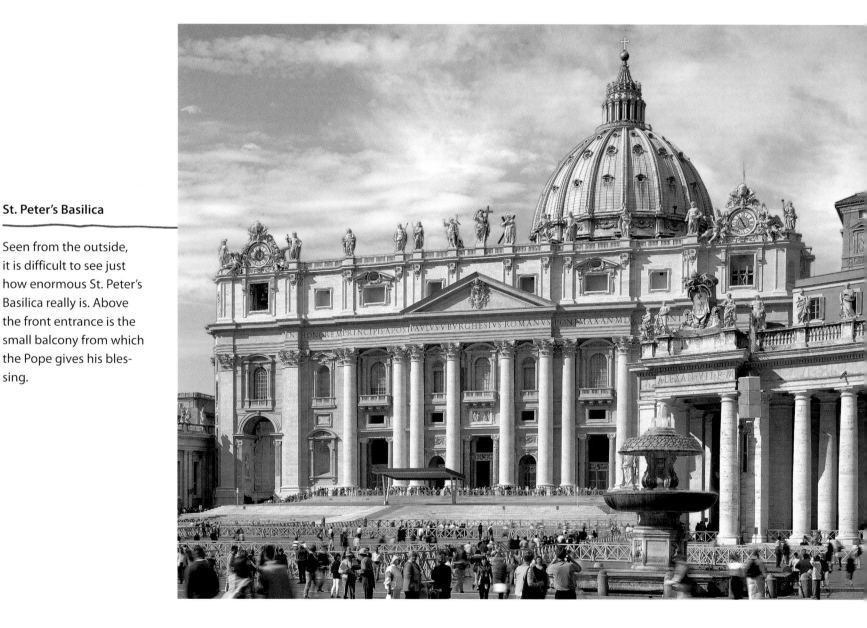

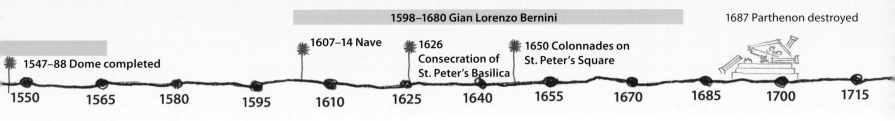

1598–1680 Gian Lorenzo Bernini

1687 Parthenon destroyed

1607–14 Nave

1626
Consecration of
St. Peter's Basilica

1650 Colonnades on
St. Peter's Square

1547–88 Dome completed

1550   1565   1580   1595   1610   1625   1640   1655   1670   1685   1700   1715

St. Peter's Basilica

The cathedral of Rome in the Vatican City: Many famous artists and architects worked on this basilica*.

As long ago as 324 CE, Constantine the Great had a church built over the grave of the apostle St. Peter. Because this old basilica did not seem grand enough to Pope Julius 1200 years later, he simply had it demolished. In its place, he had a monumental new building constructed.

St. Peter's Basilica, the Pope's church, is one of the largest in the world. 60,000 people can attend mass here at the same time. That is six times as many people as fit into Notre Dame. An enormous dome was built above the tomb of the first pope: St. Peter.

A great many architects and sculptors were involved on the construction. One of the most famous was Michelangelo.

⊿ Entrance

2 St. Peter's tomb

Started:
April 18, 1506
Location:
Vatican City (a city-state in Rome, Italy)
Architects:
Bramante, Raphael, Michelangelo, Bernini, and many others
Length:
211 m (692 feet)
Height:
132 m (433 feet)
Diameter of the dome:
43 m (141 feet)
Styles:
Renaissance, Baroque
Special features:
With a surface area of 15,000 m² (161,400 ft²) St. Peter's is one of the biggest churches in the world

Ground plan*

The ground plan was originally in the shape of a Greek cross, which has four "arms" of equal length. The length of the nave* converted it to a Latin cross.

21

The Planners' Clever Tricks

The square in front of the church was planned by Gian Lorenzo Bernini. It is oval in shape with a long trapezoid* addition leading to the basilica. The colonnades, four columns deep, line the square. When you stand in certain places, it looks as though there is just one row of columns as the others are hidden behind the first row. Through this use of the principles of perspective*, the basilica appears closer than it actually is, and the façade and dome look even higher than they are. Normally, things which are further away appear smaller. The planners avoided this effect by widening Saint Peter's Square at the end closest to the basilica. Optical illusions such as these were commonly used in Baroque architecture.

This bronze baldachin*

was built by Gian Lorenzo Bernini and Francesco Borromini. It stands above the tomb of the apostle Saint Peter. The columns alone are almost 30 meters (98 feet) high! Now you can imagine just how enormous the space is.

The mighty dome*

is the work of the famous artist Michelangelo. The interior is decorated with mosaics.

Tip
A staircase leads to the top of the dome. If you climb up it, you can see how the dome is constructed. And the view from the lantern* is worth the effort!

Michelangelo's Pietà

Of course, St. Peter's Basilica was also furnished with great works of art. One of them is this sculpture by Michelangelo. He was just 25 years old when he carved Mary mourning the dead Jesus out of a block of marble. Don't the folds look just like real fabric?

23

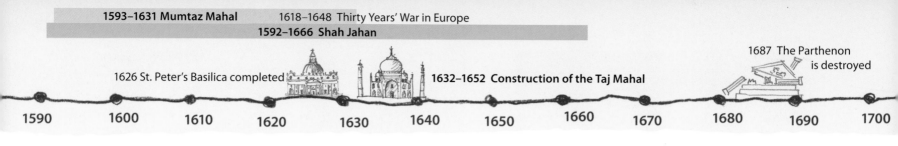
The Taj Mahal

A declaration of love made of marble and precious stones: The Taj Mahal is a tomb that looks like a palace.

Started:
1632
Construction time:
20 years
Location:
Agra, India
Comissioned (and probably designed) by:
Mughal Emperor Shah Jahan
Size:
(marble platform)
100 x 100 m
(328 x 328 ft)
Height of dome:
65 m (213 feet)
Material:
Brick covered in marble
Special features:
An image of paradise

The Taj Mahal, the "crown palace" of India, stands in its paradisiacal gardens like a white fairy-tale castle from "A Thousand and One Nights." The romantic ruler Shah Jahan wanted to create a unique memorial for his great love, Mumtaz Mahal, after her death. This is why he planned this magnificent mausoleum* made of white marble, the Taj Mahal.

He had actually planned to construct a corresponding mausoleum for himself, all in black, on the other side of the river. but, because he had used up all his money to build the Taj Mahal, his son placed him under house arrest—or rather palace arrest—and he could only gaze at his great love's tomb through the windows. At least he was buried next to her after he died.

Decorations made of precious stones

The intricate inlaid decorations made of precious stones are writings from the Koran. This is because images of animals and humans are not allowed in Islamic art.

24

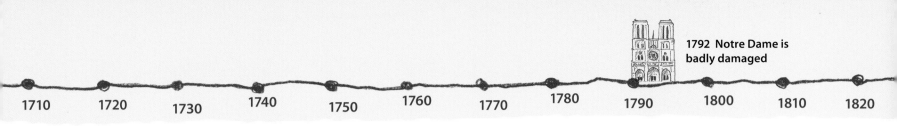

The Taj Mahal

The enormous marble-clad building stands on a gigantic marble platform. The towers at each of the four corners lean slightly outwards so that they won't fall onto the mausoleum in the event of an earthquake.

Tip

Under www.taj-mahal. net you can take a virtual tour of this fascinating building and get an idea of the unbelievable workmanship.

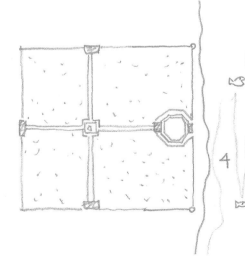

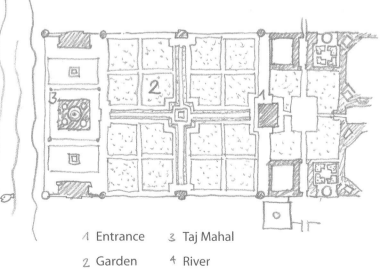

1 Entrance   3 Taj Mahal
2 Garden   4 River

Paradise on Earth

The gardens that surround the Taj Mahal were supposed to represent the Gardens of Paradise, but sadly an English governor replaced the fragrant flowers with lawns. What a shame!

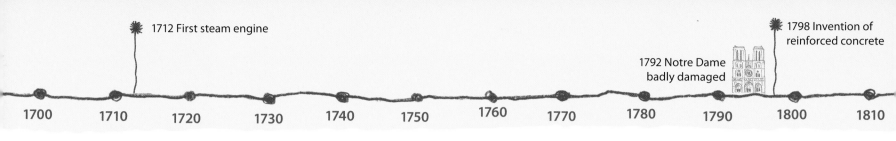

Neuschwanstein Castle

The castle was built to
plans drawn up by a
theatrical set designer.
No wonder that Walt
Disney modelled his
Cinderella Castle on
Neuschwanstein!

26

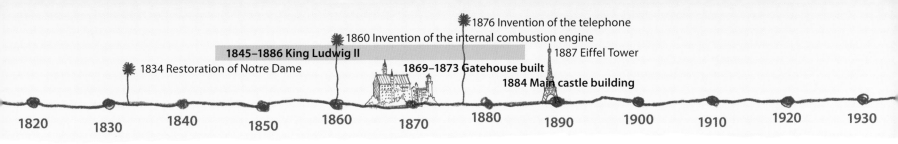

1876 Invention of the telephone
1860 Invention of the internal combustion engine
1845–1886 King Ludwig II
1887 Eiffel Tower
1834 Restoration of Notre Dame
1869–1873 Gatehouse built
1884 Main castle building

1820 1830 1840 1850 1860 1870 1880 1890 1900 1910 1920 1930

Neuschwanstein Castle

A royal home for justs 176 days! King Ludwig spent less than six months in his romantic Neuschwanstein Castle.

The three fairy-tale castles built by King Ludwig II of Bavaria are famous throughout the world: Linderhof, Herrenchiemsee, and Neuschwanstein.

Virtually every tourist who visits Germany goes to see at least one of these Bavarian castles. And so, during the main tourist season, some 12,000 feet trample through the enchanting castle, built in a medieval style, every day. Whatever would King Ludwig II say if he knew! After all, the king was so shy that he converted what was supposed to be a guest room into a beautiful but useless ceremonial room.

A number of modern technical innovations, such as a flush toilet, are tucked away in Neuschwanstein Castle, which looks like a Romanesque castle. These allowed the king to indulge in his romantic dreams while remaining very comfortable. For a few months, at least….

Started:
September 5, 1869
Construction time:
15 years, although it is still incomplete today
Location:
near Füssen, Southern Germany
Comissioned by:
King Ludwig II of Bavaria
Architect:
Eduard Riedel after a design by Christian Jank
Material:
Brick with stone cladding
Style:
Neo-Romanesque*
Special features:
Contains Germany's first water closet

1 Lower courtyard

2 Upper courtyard

3 Gatehouse

4 Main castle building

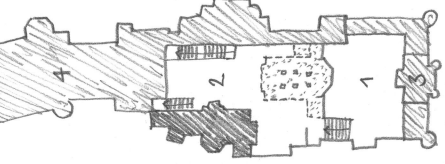

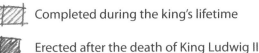 Completed during the king's lifetime

 Erected after the death of King Ludwig II

Planned (Chapel)

Ground plan*

After the gatehouse and the main part of the castle had been finished, Ludwig could move into his palace. Other buildings that were planned were never completed.

Inside the castle

Here you can see where the king's apartments were within the castle. Because the kitchen was three stories below the dining room, the king's meals were hauled up and down using a pulley system.

The Unhappy Fairy-tale King

Ludwig II became king of Bavaria at the tender age of 18. Perhaps the burden of this responsibility was too heavy for him to carry. He dreamed more and more of an ideal world and forgot the everyday reality around him. Eventually he started to sleep during the daytime and was up and about at night. He would dress up in historical costumes and be driven around the moonlit countryside in magnificent coaches. Or he would have elaborate meals with people who had died long before and were, of course, not really present. To do this, he commissioned a "magic table" that was pulled up through a trap door, already laid with delicious food from the kitchens below. And so the solitude in which he chose to live was not even interrupted by servants.

Because he spent all Bavaria's money on art and buildings and neglected the affairs of state, he was finally deposed and placed under house arrest. Ludwig II and his psychiatrist drowned mysteriously in Lake Starnberg in 1886. Nobody knows whether he was attempting to escape, or whether he ended his own life.

Neuschwanstein in 1886, the year Ludwig II died

Quiz
Which two rulers, both of whom are introduced in this book, were placed under house arrest because of their building mania?
(Answer on page 46)

Tip
You can find the opening times and lots of amazing photographs of all the rooms on the website www. neuschwanstein.com

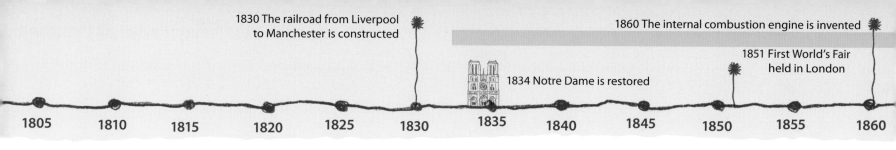
The Eiffel Tower

Whenever you think of Paris, you think of the Eiffel Tower. When it was built to mark the great World's Fair in 1889, nobody would ever have thought that it would become the city's most famous landmark. Its main opponents criticized it as an "ugly lamp post"!

Started:
  January 28, 1887
Construction time:
  2 years
Location:
  Paris, France
Built by:
  Gustave Eiffel
Architect:
  Stephan Sauvestre
Height:
  300 meters (984 feet) without antenna
Material:
  Steel (iron is the outdated term)
Style:
  Functionalism*
Special features:
  2.5 million rivets hold the tower together

Of course, we must remember that people's taste was different in those days. At about the same time, King Ludwig II was building Neuschwanstein Castle in the style of a medieval* castle. In fact, historical building styles were very fashionable at the time, so that many old forms were frequently copied in architecture.

And then Gustave Eiffel came along and built this metal structure in the middle of Paris—a tower of steel components, just the bare skeleton without anything to cover it! But Mr. Eiffel got his own way. He paid for the tower himself—and created Paris's most famous landmark.

It was originally planned that the Eiffel Tower would be dismantled again after twenty years. but it turned out to be an excellent radio antenna, and so they left it standing.

To prevent the tower from rusting it has to be painted regularly. It takes about 60 tonnes of paint to do so! What color would you paint the tower?

30

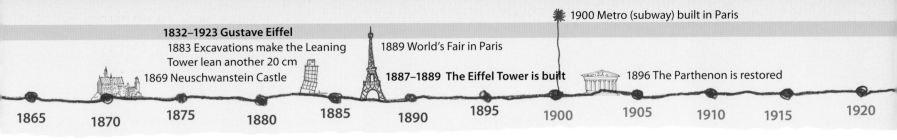

1832–1923 Gustave Eiffel

1883 Excavations make the Leaning
Tower lean another 20 cm

1869 Neuschwanstein Castle

1889 World's Fair in Paris

1887–1889 The Eiffel Tower is built

1896 The Parthenon is restored

1900 Metro (subway) built in Paris

1865   1870   1875   1880   1885   1890   1895   1900   1905   1910   1915   1920

The Eiffel Tower

The three observation platforms are 57 meters (187 feet), 115 meters (377 feet) and 276 meters (905 feet) above the ground. It's a good job there's an elevator!

Bare steel

did not appeal at all to many people at that time. The round arches between the four feet had to be added after the tower had been built, to make the "Iron Lady" look a bit prettier.

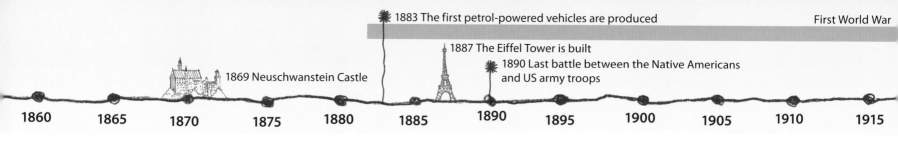

1883 The first petrol-powered vehicles are produced

First World War

1887 The Eiffel Tower is built

1890 Last battle between the Native Americans and US army troops

1869 Neuschwanstein Castle

1860 1865 1870 1875 1880 1885 1890 1895 1900 1905 1910 1915

The Chrysler Building

Its gleaming metal top makes this skyscraper stand out from all the others.

32

1914–1918

Second World War 1939–1945

1969 The first man on the moon

1882–1954 William van Alen

1956 Guggenheim Museum
1959 Sydney Opera House

1930/31 Empire State Building

1928–1930 Chrysler Building

1920   1925   1930   1935   1940   1945   1950   1955   1960   1965   1970   1975

The Chrysler Building

The Chrysler Building won the competition to become the tallest building in the world—by playing a trump card.

The story of the Chrysler Building is like a detective story with a comic twist. After the invention of the steel skeleton structure for tall buildings (see box on next page) it seemed as if the sky were the limit. The automobile manufacturer Chrysler decided to build the tallest skyscraper in New York—but unfortunately the head of the Bank of Manhattan had the same idea too!

And so an exciting neck-and-neck race began. Shortly before the two buildings were completed it looked as if the Bank of Manhattan building (283 meters/928 feet) was going to be one meter (3.28 feet) taller than the Chrysler Building (282 meters/925 feet). However, the architect of the Chrysler Building had a trump card hidden away out of sight: Inside the building he had secretly screwed together and stored the 56-meter (184-foot) stainless steel top of the building.

It only took a few hours to mount the crowning glory on top of the Chrysler Building, which was now even taller than the Eiffel Tower. Millionaires can be remarkably childish at times! However, the Chrysler Building's luck did not last long: Within a year, the Empire State Building had set a new record at 381 meters (1250 feet). The head of the Bank of Manhattan must have found it hard not to laugh out loud.

Started:
September 19, 1928
Construction time:
2 years
Location:
New York, USA
Built by: Chrysler Ltd.
Architect:
William van Alen
Height:
319 meters (1046 feet)
Style: Art Deco*
Material:
Reinforced concrete* with a cladding of stone and stainless steel
Special features:
Decorations in the shape of car parts

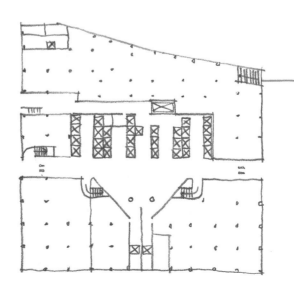

Ground plan*

There are 34 elevators in the Chrysler Building. Skyscrapers like this would probably never have been built if elevators had not been invented. Just imagine what it would be like to live on the 71st floor and have to quickly empty the trash can!

⊠ = Elevator

33

Waterspouts

These decorative characters high up on the side of the building are shaped like figures on a car radiator.

Quiz

Do you know when similar waterspouts or gargoyles were used?

(Solution on p. 46)

Scraping the Sky

When you were younger, did you pile up bricks higher and higher until the tower fell down? Adults like to build tall buildings too. When the industrial production of steel was invented about 150 years ago, architects could really let their imagination run wild! The material was relatively light and permitted stable steel skeletons to be built which could then be filled out with concrete or bricks. This way of building is known as the skeleton construction method. The first skyscrapers were built in this way and this is how high-rise buildings are still constructed today.

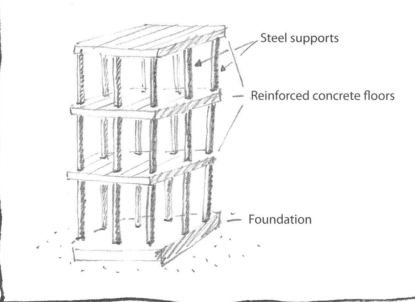

Steel supports

Reinforced concrete floors

Foundation

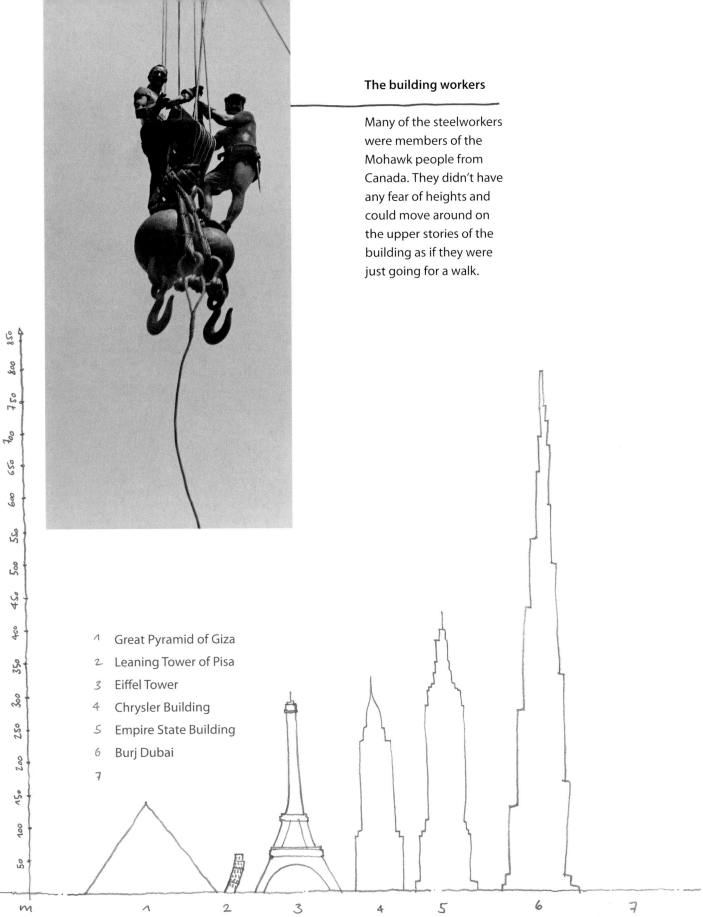

The building workers

Many of the steelworkers were members of the Mohawk people from Canada. They didn't have any fear of heights and could move around on the upper stories of the building as if they were just going for a walk.

1   Great Pyramid of Giza
2   Leaning Tower of Pisa
3   Eiffel Tower
4   Chrysler Building
5   Empire State Building
6   Burj Dubai
7

For almost 40 years the Eiffel Tower held the record as the world's tallest building, until it was overtaken by the Chrysler Building. The title is currently held by the Burj Dubai which has already reached a height of 643.3 meters (2110 feet) although it is still under construction. However, it is bound to be beaten sooner or later. How about designing your very own, even higher tower (7)?

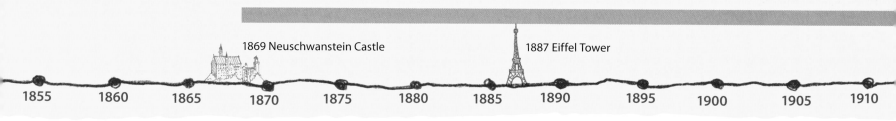
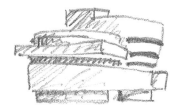

The Guggenheim Museum New York

Started:
  1956
Construction time:
  3 years
Location:
  New York, USA
Architect:
  Frank Lloyd Wright
Materials:
  Reinforced concrete*
Style:
  Classical Modernism*
Special features:
  A novel way to present art

"A washing machine full of art": The architect had to put up with a lot of criticism because of his unusual building.

Artists who branch out in a completely new direction are often laughed at or even insulted. So the architect Frank Lloyd Wright was used to being criticized. He is regarded as being one of the forerunners of Classical Modernism* and he was famous for designing buildings unlike anything that had ever been seen before. That was the very reason why the director of the Solomon R. Guggenheim Foundation asked Mr Wright to design a museum for its magnificent collection of modern art. The client and architect soon agreed on a circular shape, but it still took thirteen years and many, many revisions before the City of New York approved the plans and a builder had been found who was able to carry out the complicated design in reinforced concrete. Frank Lloyd Wright died one year before the museum finally opened. What a pity, because the "washing machine" is still one of the world's finest museums.

Interior

Solomon R. Guggenheim's art collection is shown along a long, spiral-shaped ramp* which visitors simply walk down. Beforehand they are allowed to take the elevator to the top!

36

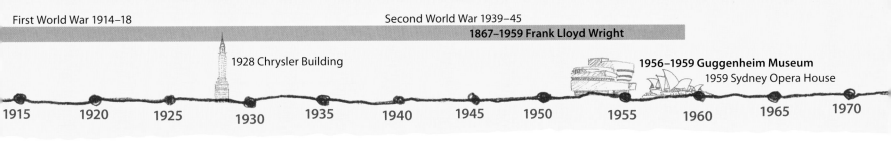
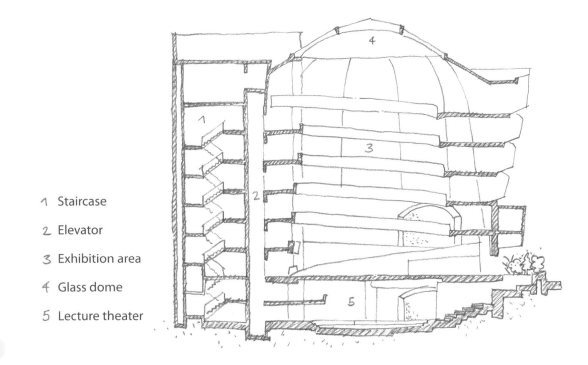

The Guggenheim Museum

looks like a sculpture itself. Some critics even felt that it stole the show from the works of art on display.

1 Staircase

2 Elevator

3 Exhibition area

4 Glass dome

5 Lecture theater

Cross-section*

It was not at all easy to find someone who could manufacture the sections of reinforced concrete* which get progressively wider towards the top. In the middle there is an open rotunda* which is lit by a glass dome*.

The Sydney Opera House

The roofs of the Sydney Opera House look like rows of white sails lying on the shore. Or are they more like shells or perhaps even nuns' hats? What does the shape remind you of?

Cross-section*

Here you can see where the different rooms are in the building.

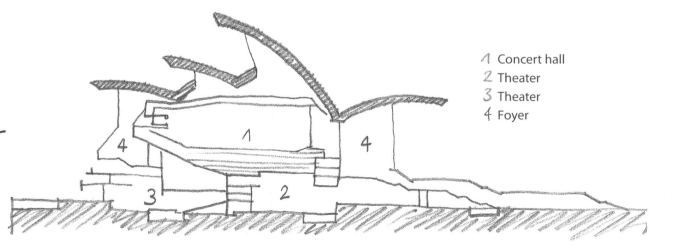

1 Concert hall
2 Theater
3 Theater
4 Foyer

38

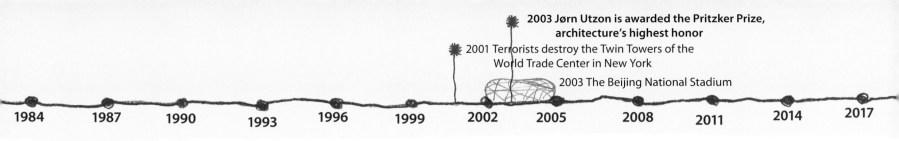
The Sydney Opera House

Melon skins or sharks' fins? The shells that cover the Sydney Opera House look like anything but normal roofs!

Some of the greatest buildings have caused the biggest arguments, most of which were about money. This was also the case with the Sydney Opera House: Because of their complicated shell shape, the roofs cost 100 million Australian dollars. Originally, they had been estimated at just 7 million!

The Danish architect Jørn Utzon left Australia after just half of the construction time was up and was not even invited to the inauguration. He was so annoyed that he took the plans for the interior work with him.

The reconciliation finally took place 43 years later. Jørn Utzon and his son were commissioned to work out the basis of future developments and possible alterations. At last, the building's "real father" was in charge of his shell-shaped opera house again!

Started:
March 2,1959
Construction time:
14 years
Location:
Sydney, Australia
Architect:
Jørn Utzon
Surface area:
183 m x 118 m
(600 x 387 feet)
Height:
67 m
Materials:
Reinforced concrete*;
roofs covered with
ceramic tiles
Special features:
Australia's best-
known building and
one of its symbols

1 Concert hall
2 Opera
3 Restaurant

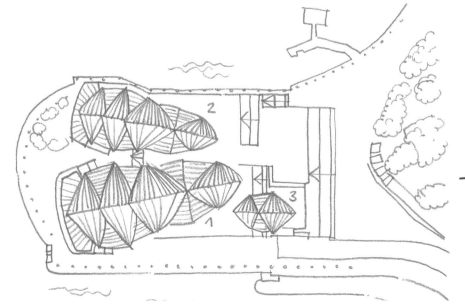

The Opera House

is located on a peninsula
in Sydney harbor.

The Roofs

Over one million white-glazed ceramic tiles from Sweden were flown half way around the world to Australia.

The bright white roofs look almost as though they had been folded out of sheets of paper, don't they? Architects often use models, which give you a good overview of the overall effect. If you like, you can make your own opera house using stiff paper, scissors and glue! You can also use cardboard tubes or small boxes. Would you make your opera house colorful or pure white like in Sydney?

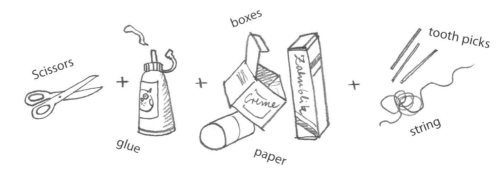

Scissors + glue + boxes paper + tooth picks string

The Platform Principle

Jørn Utzon traveled all over the world and was familiar with the architecture of many cultures. He particularly liked old temple complexes. Sometimes all that is left of them is the plinth. He said about them that: "As an architectural element, the platform is fascinating. I lost my heart to it on a trip to Mexico.... You feel the firm ground beneath you, as if you were standing on a great cliff." Jørn Utzon created his own "cliff" in Sydney. Visitors can enjoy the art on top of the platform while preparations for the evening performance are made below.

The Orange Principle

The curvatures caused quite a headache for the structural engineers* working on the building. Until Jørn Utzon came up with the idea of the orange: the individual sections of the roof are like orange segments. In other words, they are different-sized segments of an enormous hollow ball. That means that the curvature of the supporting iron structures in the concrete is always the same and really easy to calculate.

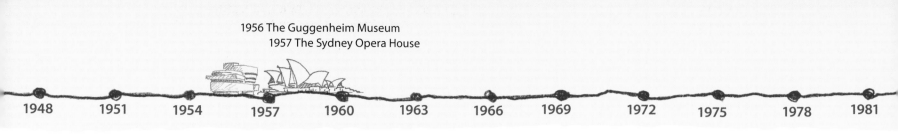

The Beijing National Stadium

Started:
2003
Construction time:
5 years
Location:
Beijing, China
Architects:
Jacques Herzog and
Pierre de Meuron
with the artist
Ai Wei Wei
Length:
320 m (1050 feet)
Height: 69,2 m (227
feet)
Material:
Steel, concrete, and
synthetic materials
Special features:
To cut costs, the plan-
ned sliding roof was
dropped

Birds build nests. And sometimes humans do, too:
the National Stadium for the Olympic Games in Beijing
looks like a bird's nest.

Up to 10,000 construction workers worked on the building site of the
National Stadium in Beijing at the same time. When the pyramids were
being built it must have looked something like this, too! But the result is
quite different: While the pyramids were built to keep intruders out, the
Olympic Stadium is designed to welcome visitors and symbolizes China's
efforts to open up politically. That is why the two Swiss architects Herzog
and de Meuron designed such an irregular and see-through nest structure.

The network of steel girders surrounds a large concrete bowl that holds
the 91,000 seats and the sports tracks. Because the outer structure can
become warped by heat, the outer and inner
structures are not connected to one another. Transparent synthetic sheeting
between the steel girders at the top
ensure that the spectators stay
dry even if it rains. Most birds
can only dream of such luxury!

The steel girders

are all welded to
each other. Virtually
all the individual pieces
are different shapes and
sizes and weigh up to 350
tonnes.

42

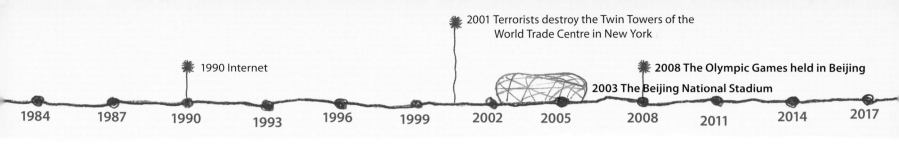

The Beijing National Stadium

The architects were not thinking about a bird's nest when they designed it. It was given its nickname later. What does the shape remind you of?

What would the bird sitting in this nest look like? Why not try to draw it?

Glossary

ANTIQUITY This refers to a period in ancient history centered around the Mediterranean Sea. Classical Antiquity lasted from around 1200 BCE to 600 CE, when culture was dominated by Ancient Greece and the Roman Empire.

ARCHEOLOGIST Somebody who studies ancient art and culture, often going on digs or excavations to uncover lost sites.

ART DECO A style that was fashionable around 1920, particularly in Paris. Fabrics, furniture and even buildings were decorated with intricate (plant) patterns.

ASYMMETRICAL When something has two halves that are exactly the same, it is called symmetrical. The opposite is called asymmetrical, even if the differences are very small.

BALDACHIN A roof made of fabric or another material that is only supported by its corners on columns or pillars. You often find baldachins above altars in churches or above thrones.

BAROQUE A style that flourished in Europe between about 1575 and 1770. Baroque decoration is very elaborate and "flashy." Houses and furniture with lots of gold and ornamentation are often from the baroque period.

BASILICA A large and important church that has been given special ceremonial rites by the Pope. Architecturally, the interior is divided lengthways by rows of columns into at least three sections. The central section, called the nave, has a higher ceiling than the aisles on either side. Some basilicas are divided into more than three sections.

CATHEDRAL A cathedral is a church headed by a bishop. Cathedrals are usually very big and impressive.

CROSS SECTION An architectural drawing of a building cut in half either crosswise or lengthwise so that you can see what it is like inside. It's rather like looking into a dolls' house.

DOME Also known as a cupola, a dome is a high, arched, circular roof on a building.

FLOOR PLAN If you were to look at a building's walls from above (and through its roof!), you would be able to see its floor plan.

FOUNDATION The part of a building that carries the structure's entire weight. The foundation is usually beneath ground level.

FUNCTIONALISM An architectural style that doesn't have any decoration. Everything that is necessary for the house to "function" well can be visible, but nothing else. This style became fashionable around 1930.

GOTHIC A style that developed in France around 1150. It is easily to recognise thanks to the pointed arches. Enormous cathedrals that seem to grow up into the sky and have big, colorful glass windows are typical of Gothic architecture.

GOVERNOR The governor is the person who is in charge in the reigning ruler's absence.

LANTERN A small addition on top of a dome. Light enters the dome through windows in the sides of the lantern. After all, you couldn't just make a hole in the dome or else the rain would come in!

LATE ROMANESQUE see Romanesque

MAUSOLEUM A magnificently burial site is called a mausoleum, after King Mausolus (377–353 BCE). This ruler's impressive tomb was once one of the Seven Wonders of the Ancient World.

MIDDLE AGES, MEDIEVAL The period between Classical Antiquity and the Modern Age, i.e. from about 500 to 1500 CE.

MODERNISM   Modernism is a style in art and architecture that first appeared in the early 20th century. Unlike other fashions, it was as simple and straightforward as possible.

NAVE AND TRANSEPT   Churches often have a cross-shaped floor plan. The long section of the cross, in which the pews or seats are usually placed, is known as the nave. The "arms" of the cross make up the transept, where sometimes side altars can be found.

NEOCLASSICISM   A style in art and architecture between 1770 and 1830. Neoclassicism imitates the style of Greek Antiquity.

PERSPECTIVE   The appearance of buildings in relation to each other depending on where you are standing. By understanding the "laws of perspective," architects can play tricks with how we see things.

PLUMB LINE   If you hang a weight on a piece of string and wait until it has stopped swinging, the string will form an absolutely vertical line towards the ground. This is known as a plumb line or plummet.

PROPORTION   Proportion is the relationship between different measures, such as length and breadth. If something is 1.5 m long and 50 cm wide or, for example, 9 feet tall and 3 feet deep, the proportions are 3:1.

RAMP   In order to get to a higher level, you can use stairs, but often a smooth path that does not ascend too steeply is sometimes more suitable. And that is what a ramp is.

REINFORCED CONCRETE   Once steel could be produced in factories, it was soon discovered that a steel frame could be used to make concrete stronger. That was around 1900, and "reinforced concrete" has been used to build houses ever since.

RENAISSANCE   A style that developed around the 15th and 16th centuries in Europe. This was the first time that stylistic elements from Greek Antiquity were used again. "Renaissance" means "re-birth" in French.

ROMANESQUE   A style that developed between 1000 and 1250. In contrast to the Gothic style, which followed it, Romanesque churches and other buildings have round arches and appear heavier and darker.

ROMANESQUE REVIVAL
"Revival" means "bringing back to life." Around 1900, many artists and architects tried to copy old styles again. When they worked in the Romanesque style, the result is called Romanesque Revival.

ROTUNDA   A rotunda is any building with a circular ground plan.

STRUCTURAL ENGINEER   A structural engineer is somebody who works out how thick a wall or a steel girder needs to be so that a building does not collapse under a certain weight. Structural engineering is an independent profession and structural engineers and architects always work together when designing a big building.

TRAPEZOID   A trapezoid, or trapezium, is a geometric shape. It is basically a square that has been squashed so that only two sides are parallel (i.e. an equal distance apart in every place), but one side is shorter than the other.

TRANSEPT   see Nave

Answers to the quiz:

Page 7: The roofs of church towers and some houses are shaped like pyramids, for example.

Page 11: The Parthenon is a Doric temple.

Page 17: The Leaning Tower of Pisa is 54 m high nowadays.

Page 29: Mughal Emperor Shah Jahan and King Ludwig II are the two rulers who were placed under house arrest because of their building mania.

Page 34: Gargoyles are typical of the Gothic style, as you can see from Notre Dame de Paris.

Library of Congress Control Number: 2008943393, British Library Cataloguing-in-Publication Data: a catalogue record for this book is available from the British Library; Deutsche Nationalbibliothek holds a record of this publication in the Deutsche National-bibliografie; detailed bibliographical data can be found under: http://dnb.ddb.de

Photo credits: Akg-images, Berlin: pp. 4, 10, 23 top left, 37 (Rainer Grosskopf); Bildagentur Huber, GAP/Giovanni Simeone: p. 20; Jérome Blum: p. 13 left; Hervé Champol-lion: p. 8; Corbis, Düsseldorf/Richard Hamilton Smith: frontispiece; Michael Freeman: p. 36; Herbert Hartmann: p. 14; Courtesy of Herzog & de Meuron: pp. 42, 43; LAIF: pp. cover, 19, 31 left, 38; Werner Scholz: p. 25; Softeis: p. 26; Martin Thomas: p. 23 top right; Ullstein – Bonn-Sequenz: p. 32

Front cover: The Great Pyramid of Giza (p. 4); Sydney Opera House (p. 38); The Tower of London (p. 18)
Frontispiece: The Chrysler Building (p. 32)

Prestel books are available worldwide. Please contact your nearest bookseller or one of the following addresses for information concerning your local distributor.

Prestel Verlag, Munich
a member of Verlagsgruppe Random House GmbH
www.prestel.de

Prestel Publishing Ltd.
14-17 Wells Street
London W1T 3PD

Prestel Publishing
900 Broadway, Suite 603
New York, NY 10003

www.prestel.com

All drawings are by Annette Roeder

Translation: Jane Michael, Munich
Copyediting: Christopher Wynne, Bad Tölz

Project management and editing: Doris Kutschbach
Design: Michael Schmölzl, agenten.und.freunde, Munich
Production: Astrid Wedemeyer, Carolina Fahrentholz
Origination: ReproLine mediateam, Munich
Printing and binding: Printer Trento, Trento

Verlagsgruppe Random House FSC® N001967
The FSC®-certified paper *Condat matt Périgord* has been supplied by Papier Union.

ISBN 978-3-7913-4171-2